Home Maths Ages 7–8

Anita Straker

CAMBRIDGE
UNIVERSITY PRESS

1

Ask an adult to time you.
You need pencil and paper. Write only the answers.

1 Add 8 and 5.
2 Half of 10.
3 6 + 6.
4 13 take away 4.
5 7×2.
6 $10 + \square = 19$.
7 Twelve minus five.
8 3 balls at 20p each cost … ?
9 Take 10 from 26.
10 What is the total of 20p and £1?
11 $15 - 3$.
12 $12 \div 2$.
13 Write **nineteen** in figures.
14 $8 \times \square = 80$.

2

Going down

Play this with a partner.

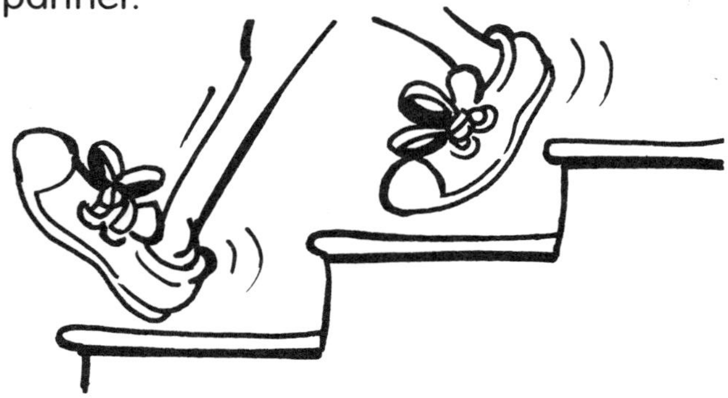

The first player chooses a multiple of 10 from 50 to 200.
(**Hint**: A multiple of 10 divides exactly by 10: for example, 80, 120, 360.)
Take turns to subtract 10, 20 or 30.
The person to reach 0 **exactly** wins.

The loser decides whether or not to go first next time.

Play at least ten times. Can you work out how to win?

Subtract multiples of 10
Work out a strategy

3

Monster

Do this with a partner.

M	O	N	S	T	E	R
1	**2**	**3**	**4**	**5**	**6**	**7**

The numbers stand for letters.

Add up in your head the numbers in the words below.

Your partner should check and say if you are right.

1 ME
2 ON
3 SO
4 ONE
5 MEN
6 NOT
7 TOE
8 SET
9 TEN
10 NOSE
11 TENT
12 MOON

Think of more words using the letters of MONSTER.

Ask your partner to work out what they are worth.

You must say if your partner is right.

Add several small numbers
Use addition facts to 20

4

15 in a line

Play with a partner.

Share a pencil and paper.

Draw a grid and sets of numbers like this.

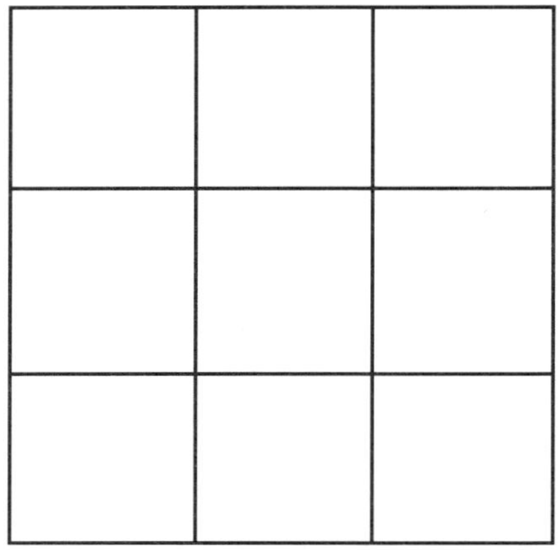

1 3 5 7 9 **2 4 6 8**

The first player uses 1, 3, 5, 7, 9.

The second player uses 2, 4, 6, 8.

Each number can be used only once.

Take turns to write one of your numbers on the grid.

Cross out the number you used.

The winner is the first to get a line of three numbers adding up to 15.

The line can be a row, column or diagonal.

Play several times.

Take turns to go first.

Add pairs of small numbers
Subtract from 15

5

Ask an adult to read you these.
You need pencil and paper. Write only the answers.

1 32 plus 10.
2 7 take away 5.
3 3 add 2 add 1.
4 2 times 5.
5 Divide 14 by 2.
6 26 minus 10.
7 Multiply 10 by 6.
8 What is 5p more than 20p?
9 Write two numbers that add up to 12.
10 Share 50 equally among 5.
11 Subtract 9 from 13.
12 Double 8.
13 Write 43 to the nearest 10.
14 Find the difference between 7 and 11.

6

Multiply

Do this on your own.

You need pencil and paper.

Choose two different numbers from this set.

2   **3**   **4**   **5**   **10**

Multiply them.

There are 10 ways to choose and 9 different answers.

Can you list them all?

Change the rules

The two numbers must be the same.

What are the different answers now?

Practise times-tables (2, 3, 4, 5, 10)
Work systematically

7

Balloons

Two, three or four people can play.
Share a pencil and paper.

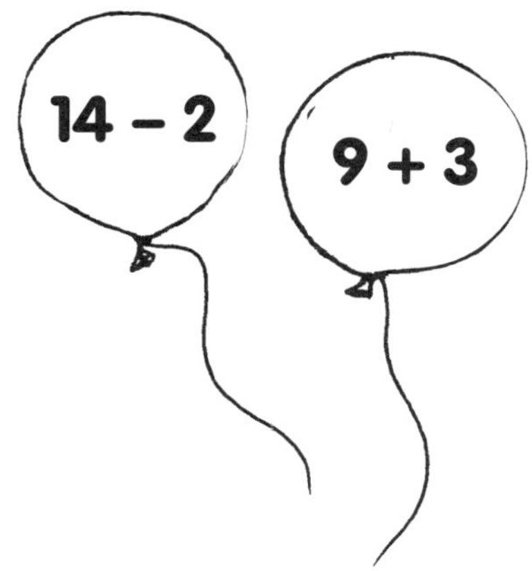

Draw a small circle in the middle of the paper.
Write 12 in the circle.

Take turns to draw a balloon.
Join it to the circle.
Write a 'sum' with an answer of 12 on your balloon.
Each one must be different.

Can you complete 24 different balloons?

Use knowledge of number facts
Think flexibly

8

Ask an adult to time you.
You need pencil and paper. Write only the answers.

1 How many tens in 90?
2 10 ÷ □ = 2.
3 7 more than 2.
4 Half of 20.
5 48 plus 10.
6 40 – □ = 10
7 Eight twos.
8 How many more is 9 than 6?
9 What must I add to 11 to make 20?
10 What is 90p and 20p altogether?
11 What is missing: 6, 8, □, 12, 14?
12 30 metres less than 100 metres.
13 4 books at £10 each cost … ?
14 4 × □ = 20.

9

Fours

Two, three or four people can play.

You need a dice.

Each player needs pencil and paper.

Each player should draw a strip like this.

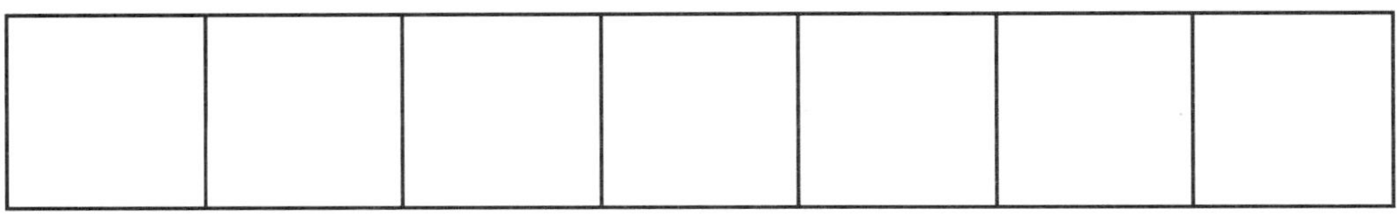

Take turns to roll the dice.

Each spot is worth 4.

Write your score on your strip.

Carry on until your strip is full.

Now take turns to roll the dice again.

Each spot is still worth 4.

If you can, cross out your score.

Otherwise wait for your next turn.

The first to cross out all their numbers wins.

Change the rules

a. Make each spot worth 10.

b. Use two dice.

Practise times-tables (4 and 10)

10

Make the most of it

Two, three or four people can play.

You need pencil and paper for each player
and a pack of playing cards.

Use the ace to 9 of each suit.

Put the cards face down in a pile.

Each player should draw this on their paper.

□ □ + □

Turn over the top card.

Everyone writes that number in one of their boxes.

No changes are allowed afterwards.

Do this two more times.

The player who makes the biggest answer wins.

Play several times.

Change the rules

a. This time try to make the smallest answer.

□ □ + □

b. Make the biggest or smallest answer using this.

□ □ – □

Understand place value
Add or subtract units to/from tens and units

11

Get rich quick

Do this with a partner.

Share a pencil and paper.

Borrow two £1 coins, two 10p coins and two 1p coins.

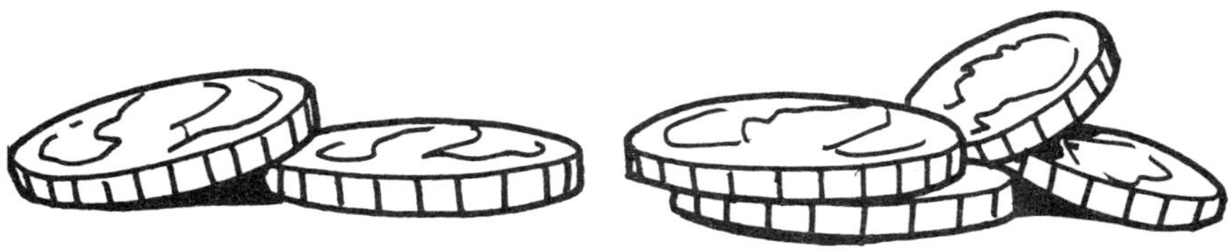

You can make £2.22 using all the coins.

You can make 25 different amounts using some but not all of the coins.

Take turns to write what they are.

Don't forget to give back the money!

Add up and record sums of money
Work systematically

12

Ask an adult to read you these.
You need pencil and paper. Write only the answers.

1 3 add 2 add 3.

2 Six twos.

3 8 less than 10.

4 5 times 3.

5 13 plus 6.

6 Double 7.

7 15 minus 4.

8 How many less than 11 is 6?

9 Write two numbers with a difference of 9.

10 What is next: 14, 16, 18, 20 … ?

11 20 metres more than 100 metres.

12 Multiply 5 by 6.

13 Write 58 to the nearest 10.

14 What must I take from 20 to leave 16?

13

Ask an adult to time you.
You need pencil and paper. Write only the answers.

1 □ + 30 = 50.

2 64 + 5.

3 2 multiplied by 7.

4 How many less than 7 is 1?

5 Is 31 odd or even?

6 39 – 7.

7 Add 11 to 20.

8 How many twos in 16?

9 8 + 7.

10 20 ÷ □ = 2.

11 What is missing: 23, □, 27, 29?

12 2 pens at 25p each cost … ?

13 14 – 9.

14 Which three coins make 9p?

14

Stick numbers

Do this on your own.

You need pencil and paper and about 15 sticks - perhaps straws cut up.

You can make stick numbers like this.
Six sticks make 0, two sticks make 1, five sticks make 2, and so on.

0 1 2 3 4 5 6 7 8 9

Which numbers use their own number of sticks?

Which numbers less than 100 use 7 sticks?

What is the highest number you can make with 7 sticks?

Understand place value
Work out a strategy

Toyshop

Do this with a partner.

Share a pencil and paper.

Look at the shop window.

You can spend £1 exactly.

What could you buy?

Each toy must be different.

There are 14 different ways to choose toys to buy.

Write as many ways as you can.

Add up money to a total of £1
Record systematically

16

Four in a line

Play with a partner.

Share a pencil and paper.

Draw a grid like this.

1	3	7	9	5	2
13	14	18	20	16	11
26	28	30	29	27	25
12	17	23	19	15	13
2	6	10	8	4	1

In turn, choose any two of these numbers.

4 5 6 7 8 9 10 13 20

Add or subtract your two numbers.

If the answer is on the grid, mark it with your initial.

You can mark each answer only once.

The winner is the first to get four of their own marks in a straight line.

The line can be in any direction.

Add or subtract pairs of numbers up to 20
Work out a strategy

17

Ask an adult to read you these.
You need pencil and paper. Write only the answers.

1 Add 9 to 61.
2 11 take away 8.
3 15 more than 20.
4 Four fours, add 1.
5 6 plus 8.
6 Half of 12.
7 How many hours in a day?
8 Nine twos.
9 Round 58 to the nearest 10.
10 How many fives in 50?
11 Write **sixty-seven** in figures.
12 One less than 60.
13 How many more than 5 is 11?
14 What is next: 28, 38, 48 … ?

18

Evens

Do this on your own.

You need a pack of playing cards, a pencil and paper.

Use the 2 to 9 of each suit.

Make 16 different even numbers.

Use all the cards.

Write your even numbers in order.

Start with the largest.

74 is even

Recognise odd and even numbers up to 100
Order two-digit numbers

19

Triples

Do this on your own.

You need pencil and paper.

12	3	6
9	7	11
5	2	8

Pick three of these numbers.

They can be the same or different.

The three numbers must total 20.

There are 10 different ways to do it.

Make a list of them all.

Add three numbers to make a total of 20
Work systematically

20

Ask an adult to time you.

You need pencil and paper. Write only the answers.

1. □ – 10 = 70.
2. Double 20.
3. □ × 5 = 40.
4. 61 + 8.
5. 9 more than 10.
6. 14 take away 8.
7. Which 3 coins make 17p?
8. How many centimetres in 1 metre?
9. Add 6 to 7.
10. Share 12 equally among 6.
11. 56 – 5.
12. What is missing: □, 56, 66, 76?
13. What is the total of £19 and £4?
14. 5 snacks at 5p each cost … ?

21

Fives and tens

Play with a partner.

You need a pack of playing cards.

Use the ace to 8 of each suit.

Put the pack face down in a pile.

The first player chooses one of these grids.

The second player has the other one.

Draw your grid on your paper.

5	35	10
50	30	80

15	70	25
40	20	60

Take turns to turn over the top card.

Each time, choose whether the spots on the card are worth 5 or 10.

If your score matches one of your numbers, cross it out.

The winner is the first to cross out all their numbers.

Play again.

Take turns to go first.

Practise times-tables (5 and 10)

22

Triplets

Two, three or four people can play.

You need a pack of playing cards.

Use the ace to 9 of each suit.

Spread the cards face down.

Take turns.

Turn over three cards.

If the total is odd, you win the three cards.

If not, turn them back.

6 + 1 + 4 = 11
11 is odd

Carry on until all the cards have been won.

The player who wins the most sets of three cards wins the game.

Change the rules

Use the 2 to 10 of each suit.

If the answer is even, you win the three cards.

Add three numbers and recognise odd numbers
Work out a strategy

Home Maths Ages 7–8 Answers

1

1	13
2	5
3	12
4	9
5	14
6	9
7	7
8	60p
9	16
10	£1.20
11	12
12	6
13	19
14	10

2

A player on 200, 160, 120, 80, 40 … should lose, if the other player plays correctly. From 40, for example, no matter whether 10, 20 or 30 is subtracted, it will not be enough to reach zero. The other player can then win on their next move.

3

1	ME	7
2	ON	5
3	SO	6
4	ONE	11
5	MEN	10
6	NOT	10
7	TOE	13
8	SET	15
9	TEN	14
10	NOSE	15
11	TENT	19
12	MOON	8

More words: TO, NO, TOO, SEE, SON, TEST, STONE …

5

1	42
2	2
3	6
4	10
5	7
6	16
7	60
8	25p
9	Any pair with a sum of 12
10	10
11	4
12	16
13	40
14	4

6

2 x 3 = 6	3 x 5 = 15
2 x 4 = 8	3 x 10 = 30
2 x 5 = 10	4 x 5 = 20
2 x 10 = 20	4 x 10 = 40
3 x 4 = 12	5 x 10 = 50

Change the rules

2 x 2 = 4
3 x 3 = 9
4 x 4 = 16
5 x 5 = 25
10 x 10 = 100

8

1	9
2	5
3	9
4	10
5	58
6	30
7	16
8	3
9	9
10	£1.10 (or 110p)
11	10
12	70 metres
13	£40
14	5

11

Amounts that can be made from two £1 coins, two 10p coins, two 1p coins

£2.22	£1.22	22p
£2.21	£1.21	21p
£2.20	£1.20	20p
£2.12	£1.12	12p
£2.11	£1.11	11p
£2.10	£1.10	10p
£2.02	£1.02	2p
£2.01	£1.01	1p
£2	£1	

12

1	8
2	12
3	2
4	15
5	19
6	14
7	11
8	5
9	Any pair differing by 9
10	22
11	120 metres
12	30
13	60
14	4

13

1	20
2	69
3	14
4	6
5	31 is odd
6	32
7	31
8	8
9	15
10	10
11	25
12	50p
13	5
14	5p, 2p, 2p

14

4, 5 and 6 use their own number of sticks.

8, 12, 21, 13, 31, 15, 51, 47, 74 each use 7 sticks.

The highest number you can make with 7 sticks is 711.

Children could extend this puzzle by inventing their own stick problems.

15

jack, ball
jack, man
teddy, robot, ball
teddy, dino, ball
teddy, robot, man
teddy, dino, man
teddy, kite, man, book
teddy, kite, ball, book
doll, robot, dino
doll, robot, kite, book
doll, dino, kite, book
robot, dino, man, ball
robot, man, ball, kite, book
dino, man, ball, kite, book

17

1	70
2	3
3	35
4	17
5	14
6	6
7	24 hours
8	18
9	60
10	10
11	67
12	59
13	6
14	58

18

The even numbers that can be made are:

98	58
96	56
94	54
92	52
78	38
76	36
74	34
72	32

19

Ways of making 20:

12, 6 and 2
12, 5 and 3
11, 7 and 2
11, 6 and 3
9, 9 and 2
9, 8 and 3
9, 6 and 5
8, 7 and 5
8, 6 and 6
7, 7 and 6

20

1	80
2	40
3	8
4	69
5	19
6	6
7	10p, 5p, 2p
8	100 centimetres
9	13
10	2
11	51
12	46
13	£23
14	25p

23

Ways to score 14 with four rolls of a dice are:

6, 6, 1, 1
6, 5, 2, 1
6, 4, 3, 1
6, 4, 2, 2
6, 3, 3, 2
5, 5, 3, 1
5, 5, 2, 2
5, 4, 4, 1
5, 4, 3, 2
5, 3, 3, 3
4, 4, 3, 3
4, 4, 4, 2

24

1	69
2	15
3	101
4	23
5	7
6	11
7	18
8	57
9	8
10	90 centimetres
11	80
12	70
13	17
14	650

25

1	25
2	20
3	40
4	102 is even
5	33
6	2p, 2p, 2p, 1p
7	36
8	40
9	10
10	£1.50 (or 150p)
11	16
12	31 days
13	45
14	12

27

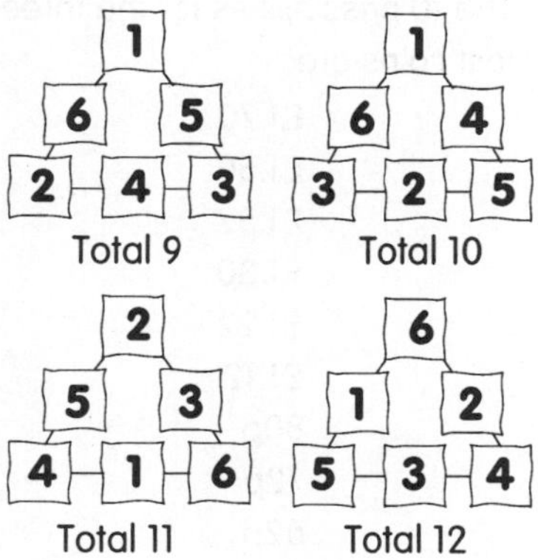

29

1	50
2	88
3	82
4	50
5	9
6	10
7	13
8	10p, 5p, 5p
9	5
10	90
11	25
12	30 days
13	30
14	Wednesday

31

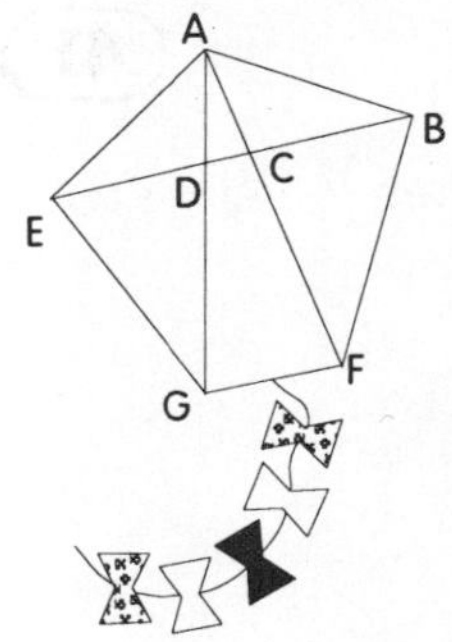

11 triangles
5 single
5 double
1 triple

ABC	ACD	AFG
ABD	ACE	BCF
ABE	ADE	DEG
ABF	AEG	

32

1	25
2	62
3	35p
4	31
5	2
6	399
7	30
8	10p, 10p, 2p, 1p
9	8 metres (or 8m)
10	£1.20
11	9
12	10
13	18
14	15p

35

Ways to score 26 with three darts:

double 6, double 6, 2
double 6, double 6, double 1
double 6, double 5, 4
double 6, double 5, double 2
double 6, double 4, 6
double 6, double 4, double 3
double 5, double 5, 6
double 5, double 5, double 3
double 5, double 4, double 4

36

1	45
2	34
3	6
4	32
5	3
6	3
7	14
8	35
9	30 kilograms (or 30 kg)
10	70 centimetres (or 70 cm)
11	901
12	19
13	11
14	9

37

1	87
2	38
3	4
4	25
5	35
6	12
7	40
8	£1.50
9	400
10	12 centimetres (or 12 cm)
11	31
12	60 minutes
13	86
14	20

38

For example,

39

1	9	AT, IS
2	7	IT
3	6	RIP
4	8	TIP, PIT, RAP, PEP
5	11	AS, PEA
6	18	SET
7	12	RAT, ART, PET, SIR
8	17	SEA, TEE
9	14	SIT, TAT
10	16	SAT, SIS
11	10	SIP, TAP, PAT
12	15	ATE, EAT, TEA

More words: PART, TRAP, PEAS, SPIT, SEAT, PEARS, STRIPE …

41

1	10
2	66
3	45 litres
4	48
5	16
6	140
7	300
8	110
9	7
10	18
11	365 days or 366 days
12	3
13	25
14	5 kilograms (or 5 kg)

42

On the farm there are:

2 rabbits
13 ducks

43

The 10 possibilities for the three lost coins are:

£1.70
£1.60
£1.52
£1.30
£1.22
£1.12
80p
72p
62p
32p

44

1	48
2	100
3	£1.50 or 150p
4	5
5	5p
6	78
7	54
8	9 kilograms (or 9 kg)
9	£60
10	60
11	20
12	£49
13	23
14	10

45

For example

1 = 6 – 5	13 = 6 + 5 + 2
2 = 2	14 = 6 + 6 + 2
3 = 5 – 2	15 = 5 + 5 + 5
4 = 6 – 2	16 = 6 + 5 + 5
5 = 5	17 = 6 + 6 + 5
6 = 6	18 = 6 + 6 + 6
7 = 5 + 2	19 = 6 + 6 + 5 + 2
8 = 6 + 2	20 = 5 + 5 + 5 + 5
9 = 5 + 2 + 2	21 = 6 + 5 + 5 + 5
10 = 5 + 5	22 = 6 + 6 + 5 + 5
11 = 6 + 5	23 = 6 + 6 + 6 + 5
12 = 6 + 6	24 = 6 + 6 + 6 + 6

23

Four rolls

Two, three or four people can play.

You need a dice for the first part and pencil and paper for the second part.

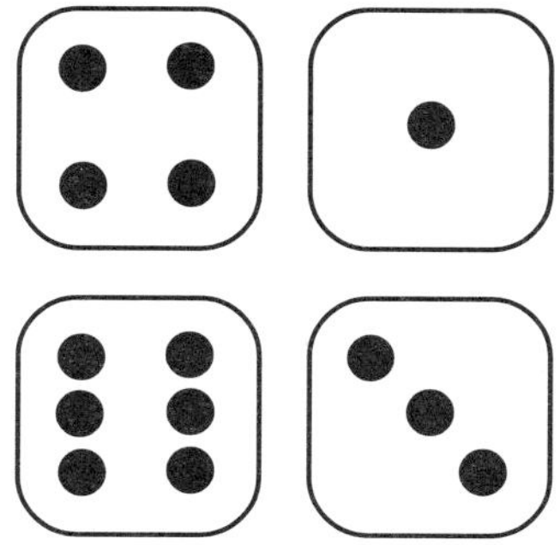

Take turns to roll the dice.

Roll it four times.

You score a point only if your four rolls add up to 14.

The winner is the first to get 2 points.

Play again. Who wins this time?

Do this part by yourself.

There are 12 different ways of getting 14 with four dice rolls.

How many of them can you find?

Add four numbers with a total up to 24
Work systematically

24

Ask an adult to read you these.
You need pencil and paper. Write only the answers.

1 71 minus 2.

2 Half of 30.

3 98 plus 3.

4 Take 6 from 29.

5 How many twos in 14?

6 9 less than 20.

7 Double 9.

8 What is next: 97, 87, 77, 67 … ?

9 Subtract 7 from 15.

10 Take 10 centimetres from 1 metre.

11 What is the sum of 50 and 30?

12 What is the product of 7 and 10?

13 8 plus 9.

14 Write in figures **six hundred and fifty**.

25

Ask an adult to time you.
You need pencil and paper. Write only the answers.

1 Half of 50.
2 14 + □ = 34.
3 20 less than 60.
4 Is 102 odd or even?
5 26 + 7.
6 Which 4 coins make 7p?
7 42 – 6.
8 Is 36 nearer to 30 or to 40?
9 7 × □ = 70.
10 3 comics at 50p each cost … ?
11 Write the product of 2 and 8.
12 How many days in May?
13 What is missing: 35, 40, □, 50?
14 □ ÷ 2 = 6.

26

Make 100

Two, three or four people can play.
You need a dice.
Each player needs pencil and paper.

Take turns to roll the dice.
If you roll, say, 5 it can be 50 or 5.
Write your score on each turn.
No changes are allowed afterwards.
Have four turns each.

30 + 2 + 60 + 5 = 97

Add up your four numbers.
The player whose score is nearest 100 wins.
Play several times.

Understand place value
Add tens and units

27

Triangles

Ask your family to join in.

You each need a pencil and piece of paper.

Share some scissors.

Each person should use their paper to make 6 number cards.

1	2	3	4	5	6

Arrange your 6 cards in a triangle shape.

Make each side of the triangle add up to 9.

Who can do it first?

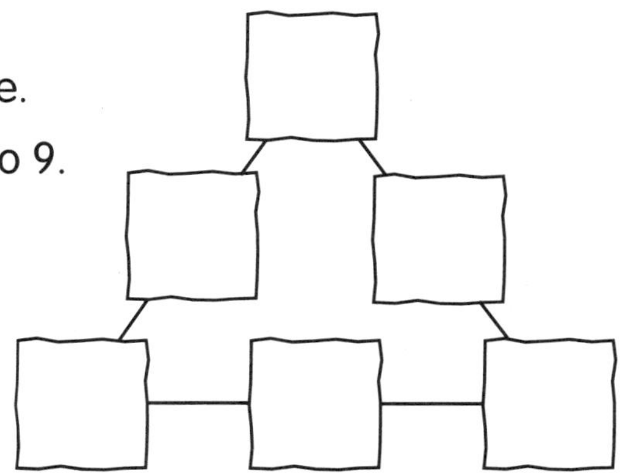

Change the rules

a. Make each side total 10.

b. Make each side total 11.

c. Make each side total 12.

Add three small numbers to total 9, 10, 11 or 12
Think logically to eliminate what won't work

28

Snake

Two, three or four people can play.

You need two dice.

Each player needs a pencil and a piece of paper.

Each player should draw a snake like this.

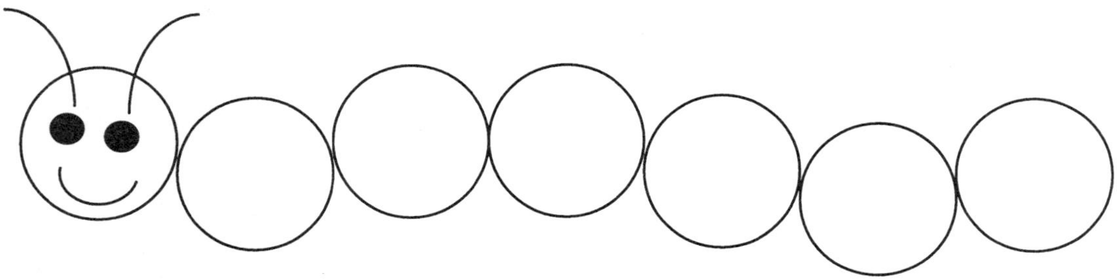

Take turns to roll both dice.

Make a two-digit number.

If you roll, say, 6 and 3 you can make 36 or 63.

Write your number in any circle on the snake.

The numbers on the snake must all be in order.

If your number will not fit in the order you miss writing a number on this turn.

The winner is the first to fill their snake with six numbers all in order.

Understand place value
Order two-digit numbers

29

Ask an adult to read you these.
You need pencil and paper. Write only the answers.

1 15 more than 35.

2 Take 5 from 93.

3 78 plus 4.

4 Double 25.

5 8 plus 4 minus 3.

6 Divide 100 by 10.

7 7 less than 20.

8 Which three coins make 20p?

9 How many fives in 25?

10 Round 92 to the nearest 10.

11 What is next: 45, 40, 35, 30 … ?

12 How many days in April?

13 Write the product of 3 and 10.

14 What is 2 days before Friday?

30

Tables

Learn your 5 times-table by heart.

Say it forwards.

Say it backwards.

Make up a tune and sing it.

Say it in the voice of an animal. Who can guess the animal?

Ask an adult to ask you questions like:

Six fives.

7 times 5.

5 multiplied by 4.

How many fives in 45?

Divide 15 by 5.

Divide 5 into 40.

Share 50 equally among 5.

How quickly can you answer?

Change the rules

a. Do the 2 times-table.

b. Do the 10 times-table.

Learn the 2, 5 and 10 times-tables by heart

31

Kite puzzle

This kite is made of lots of triangles.

Some are inside others.

How many of them can you count?

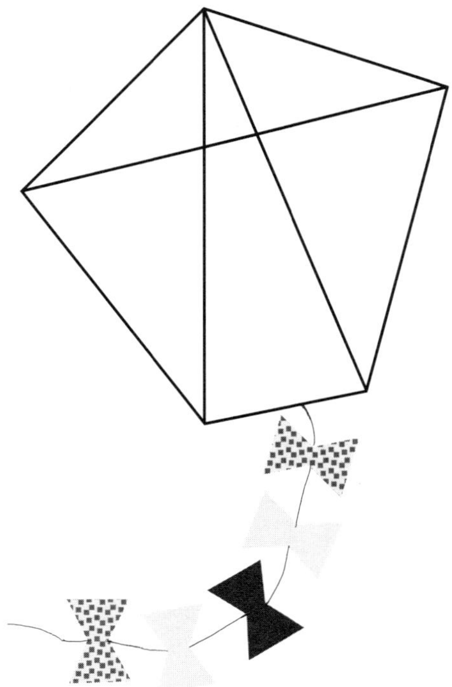

Ask your family and friends to try.

Can they find as many triangles as you can?

Recognise triangles
Work out a strategy

32

Ask an adult to time you.

You need pencil and paper. Write only the answers.

1 20 less than 45.

2 57 + 5.

3 Half of 70p.

4 □ − 3 = 28.

5 One quarter of 8.

6 One less than 400.

7 □ + 35 = 65.

8 Write 4 coins to make 23p.

9 The difference between 12m and 20m.

10 4 pencils at 30p each cost … ?

11 What is missing: 1, 5, □, 13?

12 4 × □ = 40.

13 6 + 8 + 4.

14 What change do you get from £1 for 85p?

33

Good times

Two, three or four people can play.

You need two dice.

Each player needs pencil and paper.

Each player should draw this grid.

1	2	3	4	5	6
8	9	10	12	15	16
18	20	24	25	30	36

Take turns to roll the dice.

Multiply the two numbers.

If you can, cross out the answer on your grid.

If the answer is already crossed out, your turn ends.

The first to cross out a whole row of six numbers wins.

Change the rules

The winner could be the first to get:
all four corners,
two columns of three numbers,
the whole board …

Practise times tables (up to 6 × 6)

34

Target

Two, three or four people can play.

You need 25 flat buttons (or dried beans or coins), and pencil and paper.

Draw a big grid like this.

1	1	1	1	1
2	2	2	2	2
3	3	3	3	3
4	4	4	4	4
5	5	5	5	5

Choose a target between 25 and 55.

The first player puts a button on a number and says it.

Take turns to put a button on another number.

Add on that number and say the new total.

Put only one button on each number.

The winner is the one to reach the target **exactly**.

Choose a different target and play again.

Add 1, 2, 3, 4 or 5 to a number up to 55

35

Darts

Do this on your own.

You need pencil and paper.

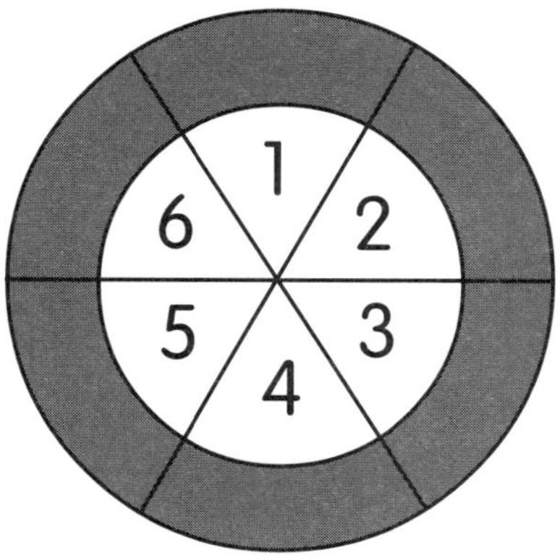

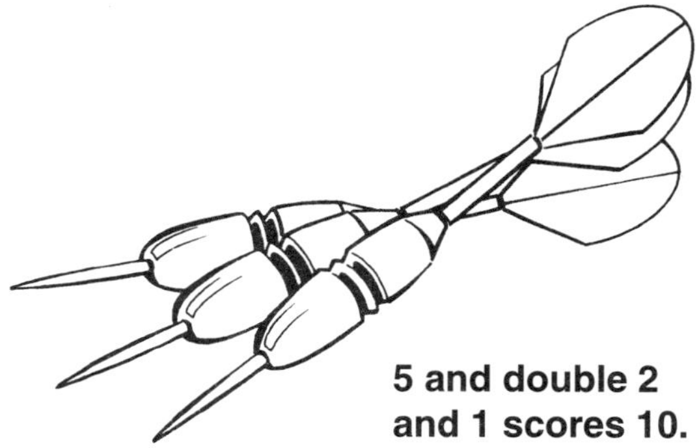

5 and double 2 and 1 scores 10.

Imagine you have 3 darts to throw at this board.

Darts in the shaded area score double.

Write nine different ways of scoring 26.

The same numbers in a different order do not count as 'different'.

Double and add small numbers
Think logically and work systematically

36

Ask an adult to read you these.
You need pencil and paper. Write only the answers.

1 Nine fives.

2 Add 6 to 28.

3 Divide 60 by 10.

4 Take 8 from 40.

5 One quarter of 12.

6 21 minus 18.

7 3 add 5 add 6.

8 15 less than 50.

9 Double 15 kilograms.

10 Take 30 centimetres from 1 metre.

11 Write in figures **nine hundred and one**.

12 Three fives, plus four.

13 What is next: 20, 17, 14 … ?

14 How many twos in 18?

37

Ask an adult to time you.

You need pencil and paper. Write only the answers.

1	78 + 9.	**8**	6 stamps at 25p each cost … ?
2	Double 19.	**9**	Multiply 100 by 4.
3	¼ of 16.	**10**	How much less than 28cm is 16cm?
4	32 – 7.	**11**	What is next: 15, 19, 23, 27 … ?
5	□ ÷ 5 = 7.	**12**	How many minutes in 1 hour?
6	2 × 3 × 2.	**13**	Add 21 to 65.
7	76 – □ = 36.	**14**	The difference between 90 and 110.

38

Coin magic

Do this on your own.

You need four of each of these coins.

Arrange the 16 coins in a 4 by 4 square.

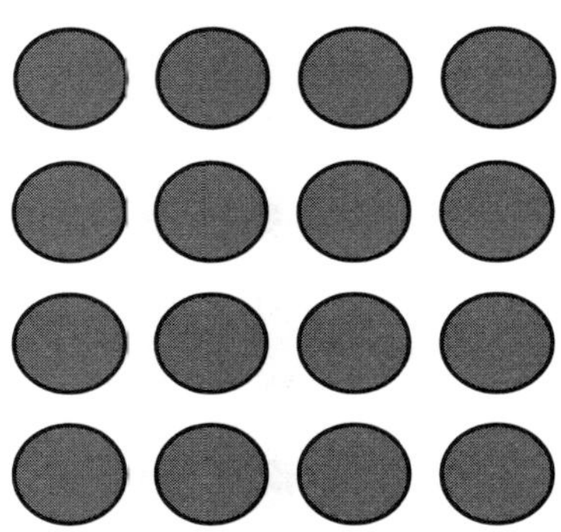

The total of each row, each column and each diagonal must be 37p.

Ask an adult to check all ten lines.

Add coins
Work out a strategy

39

Pirates

Ask all your family to join in.

P	I	R	A	T	E	S
1	**2**	**3**	**4**	**5**	**6**	**7**

Add up the numbers standing for the letters.

Find some two-letter or three-letter words that are worth these.

1	9	**5**	11	**9**	14
2	7	**6**	18	**10**	16
3	6	**7**	12	**11**	10
4	8	**8**	17	**12**	15

Secretly make a longer word using the letters of PIRATES.

Work out what it is worth and tell everyone.

Can they guess what your word is?

Add several small numbers
Use addition facts to 20

40

Splodges

Two or three people can play.

You need a dice and pencil and paper between you.

Draw these splodges on the paper.

20	16	9	17	15
14	13	25	21	6
50	12	24	40	27
18	30	8	19	35

Take turns to roll the dice.

Choose a number on a splodge.

The number you choose must divide exactly by the number you rolled.

Write your initial on that splodge.

You can initial each splodge only once.

Other players can also initial the same splodge, but only once.

If there is no new splodge for you to initial, your turn ends.

The winner is the first player to initial every splodge.

Recognise numbers in the 2, 3, 4, 5 and 6 times-tables

41

Ask an adult to read you these.
You need pencil and paper. Write only the answers.

1 90 less than 100.

2 59 add 7.

3 Half of 90 litres.

4 54 subtract 6.

5 4 times 2 times 2.

6 50 more than 90.

7 Multiply 100 by 3.

8 Write in figures **one hundred and ten**.

9 How many fives in 35?

10 What must I add to 50 to get 68?

11 How many days in one year?

12 82 minus 79.

13 5 multiplied by itself.

14 One quarter of 20 kilograms.

42

On the farm

Try this on your own.
You may need pencil and paper.

Some rabbits and ducks live on a farm.
There are 15 of them altogether.
Together they have 34 feet.
How many rabbits are there? How many ducks?

Make up another puzzle like this. Can someone in your family do it?

Recognise then add numbers in the 2 and 4 times-tables
Work out a strategy

43

How terrible!

Do this on your own.

You need pencil and paper.

Borrow one of each of these coins: £1, 50p, 20p, 10p, 2p.

Imagine you have lost three of your coins.

'How terrible!' everyone says.

'How much have you lost?'

There are 10 different possibilities.

Can you list them all?

Find the total of three coins
Record systematically

44

Ask an adult to time you.

You need pencil and paper. Write only the answers.

1. 52 – 4.
2. Divide 500 by 5.
3. 60p more than 90p.
4. 45 ÷ □ = 9.
5. 95p less than £1.
6. □ – 18 = 60.
7. 46 + 8.
8. How much more is 28kg than 19kg?
9. 4 footballs at £15 each cost … ?
10. 5 × 2 × 6.
11. ¼ of 80.
12. How much altogether is £24 and £25?
13. Find the difference between 17 and 40.
14. From the sum of 8 and 7, take 5.

45

Use only these

Play with a partner.

You need pencil and paper.

Draw this grid.

1	2	3	4	5	6
7	8	9	10	11	12
13	14	15	16	17	18
19	20	21	22	23	24

Use only these numbers and signs.

You can use them as often as you like each time.

2 5 6 + - =

Take turns to say how to make a number on the grid.

The other player checks.

If you are right, mark the number with your initial.

If not, you miss marking a number on this turn.

You can mark each number only once.

Carry on until the grid is full.

The one who marks most numbers wins the game.

Change the rules

This time use 3, 5 and 7, instead of 2, 5 and 6.

Use knowledge of addition and subtraction facts
Think flexibly

PUBLISHED BY THE PRESS SYNDICATE OF THE UNIVERSITY OF CAMBRIDGE
The Pitt Building, Trumpington Street, Cambridge CB2 1RP, United Kingdom

CAMBRIDGE UNIVERSITY PRESS
The Edinburgh Building, Cambridge CB2 2RU, United Kingdom
40 West 20th Street, New York, NY 10011-4211, USA
10 Stamford Road, Oakleigh, Melbourne 3166, Australia

First published 1998

Printed in the United Kingdom by Scotprint Ltd, Musselburgh

A catalogue record for this book is available from the British Library

ISBN 0 521 655544 paperback

Cover Illustration by Graham Round
Cartoons by Tim Sell